D1710183

Franklin School
Summit Public Schools

Incredible
Ears
Up Close

Animal
Bodies
**UP
CLOSE**

Enslow Elementary
an imprint of
Enslow Publishers, Inc.
40 Industrial Road
Box 398
Berkeley Heights, NJ 07922
USA
http://www.enslow.com

*Melissa
Stewart*

CONTENTS

WORDS TO KNOW

desert (DEH zurt)—A place that gets very little rain. The land is dry with only a few plants.

eardrum (EER druhm)—A thin, skinlike part of the ear that vibrates (moves) when noises from the air hit it.

predator (PREH duh tur)—An animal that hunts and kills other animals for food.

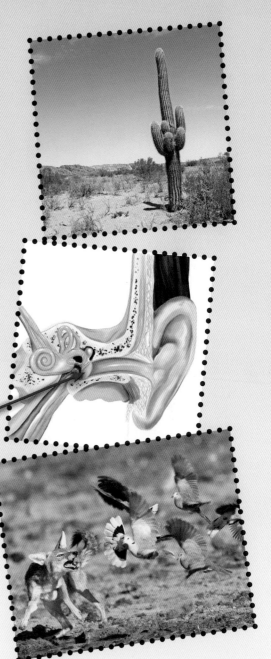

3

COTTONTAIL RABBIT

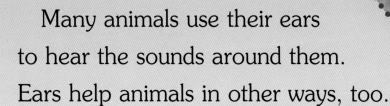

Many animals use their ears
to hear the sounds around them.
Ears help animals in other ways, too.

When a rabbit hears a **predator**, it doesn't move.
It turns its ears to find out where the sound is coming
from. Then it hops to a safe place.

4

AFRICAN ELEPHANT

UP CLOSE

An elephant has the biggest
ears on Earth. It hears VERY well.
But it also uses its ears to show how it feels.
When an elephant feels calm and safe, it holds
its ears flat against its body. But when an elephant
is angry or scared, it holds its ears out straight.

6

FENNEC FOX

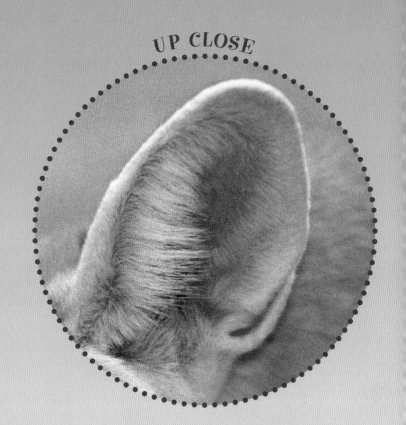

This fox lives in the hot **desert**. But it has a trick for staying cool. Heat goes out of the fox's body through the thin skin on its big ears.

NORTHERN LEOPARD FROG

See the circles behind this frog's eyes? They are its **eardrums**.

You have eardrums too. But they are deep inside your ears. Eardrums pick up noises in the air. Then they send messages to your brain so you can hear. A frog's eardrums do the same thing.

10

HIPPOPOTAMUS

UP CLOSE

Most animals have ears
on the sides of their heads.
But a hippo's ears are on top.
That's a big help on hot, sunny days.
The hippo can keep most of its body cool
in the water and still hear.

KIWI

A bird hears through holes
on the sides of its head. On most
birds, the holes are hard to see.
They are hidden under feathers.
But you can see a kiwi's ear holes.
A kiwi (KEE wee) doesn't see very well.
It uses its ears to hear predators.

UP CLOSE

HARBOR SEAL

What does a seal have in common
with a kiwi? It has ear holes too. Can you see
them? When the seal dives, the holes close tight.
That way water can't get in.

YOUR EARS

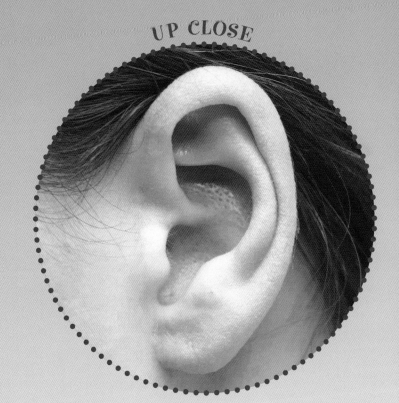

You are an animal too. Your ears help your body stay balanced. They pick up the sounds of the world around you. Your ears help you hear when a friend whispers a secret. And they warn you when a fire alarm goes off.

GUESSING GAME

1. A cricket's ears are on its . . .

2. A praying mantis has one ear on its . . .

3. A green lacewing's ears are on its . . .

4. A tiger beetle's ears are on its . . .

A. belly.

B. rear end.

C. knees.

D. wings.

(Write your answers on a piece of paper. Please do not write in this book!)

See answers on page 24.

CRICKET

PRAYING MANTIS

GREEN LACEWING

TIGER BEETLE

21

LEARN MORE

Books

Hall, Peg. *Whose Ears Are These?* Mankato, Minn.:
Picture Window Books, 2007.

Jenkins, Steve, and Robin Page. *What Do You Do
With a Tail Like This?* Boston: Houghton Mifflin, 2003.

Nunn, Daniel. *Ears*. Chicago: Heinemann-Raintree, 2007.

Stone, Lynn M. *How Do Animals Use Their Ears?*
Vero Beach, Fla.: Rourke, 2008.

WEB SITES

Did You Know There's a Jawbone in Your Ear?
<http://www.mnh.si.edu/ mammals/pages/what/ earbones.htm>

KidsHealth: Your Ears
<http://kidshealth.org/kid/ htbw/ears.html>

The Sound Site
<http://www.smm.org/sound/nocss/top.html>

INDEX

Note to Parents and Teachers: The **Animal Bodies Up Close** series supports the National Science Education Standards for K–4 science. The Words to Know section introduces subject-specific vocabulary words, including pronunciation and definitions. Early readers may need help with these new words.

Enslow Elementary, an imprint of Enslow Publishers, Inc.

Enslow Elementary® is a registered trademark of Enslow Publishers, Inc.

Copyright © 2012 by Melissa Stewart

All rights reserved.

No part of this book may be reproduced by any means
without the written permission of the publisher.

Library of Congress Cataloging-in-Publication Data
Stewart, Melissa.
  Incredible ears up close / Melissa Stewart.
    p. cm. — (Animal bodies up close)
  Includes index.
  Summary: "Discover how different animals use their ears to hear the world around them,
hide from predators, and know where they are"—Provided by publisher.
  ISBN 978-0-7660-3891-2
  1. Ear—Juvenile literature. I. Title.
  QL948.S74 2011
  591.4'4—dc22
                                        2011003338
Future editions:
Paperback ISBN 978-1-4644-0081-0
ePUB ISBN 978-1-4645-0988-9
PDF ISBN 978-1-4645-0988-6

Printed in China

012012 Leo Paper Group, Heshan City, Guangdong, China

10 9 8 7 6 5 4 3 2 1

To Our Readers: We have done our best to make sure all Internet Addresses in this book were active and appropriate when we went to press. However, the author and the publisher have no control over and assume no liability for the material available on those Internet sites or on other Web sites they may link to. Any comments or suggestions can be sent by e-mail to comments@enslow.com or to the address on the back cover.

Photo Credits: iStockphoto.com: © Jeremiah Tolbert, p. 21 (cricket), © Peter Schwarz, p. 21 (praying mantis), © Prill Mediendesign & Fotografie, p. 6; © Ken Lucas/ardea.com, p. 8; © Kim in cherl/Flickr/Getty Images, p. 1; © Michael Mährlein/Alamy, p. 9; Minden Pictures: © Chris Mattison/FLPA, p. 10, © Donald M. Jones, p. 4, © Eric Baccega/npl, p. 12, © Jim Brandenburg, p. 16, © Mark Jones, p. 15, © Norbert Wu, pp. 17, 23, © Scott Linstead/Foto Natura, p. 5, © Tim Fitzharris, p. 11, © Tony Heald/NPL, p. 3 (predator) © Tui De Roy, p. 14; Shutterstock.com, pp. 2, 3 (desert, eardrum), 7, 13, 18, 19, 21 (lacewing, tiger beetle).

Cover Photo: © Kim in cherl/Flickr/Getty Images

Series Literacy Consultant:
Allan A. De Fina, PhD
Dean, College of Education
Professor of Literacy Education
New Jersey City University
Past President of the New Jersey Reading
Association

Science Consultant:
Helen Hess, PhD
Professor of Biology
College of the Atlantic
Bar Harbor, Maine

Answers to the Guessing Game

1. Cricket: C, knees.
2. Praying mantis: A, belly.
3. Green lacewing: D, wings.
4. Tiger beetle: B, rear end.